Lobster soup with cucumbers and dried mushrooms (Ise-ebi to kyuri no soup)
Oyster miso soup (Kaki no miso shiru)

1 Lobster soup with cucumbers and dried mushrooms

Ise-ebi to kyuri no soup

Preparation time	20 minutes
Cooking time	30 minutes
To serve	4

You will need

1 medium-sized lobster
4 dried or fresh mushrooms
½ cucumber; salt
2 pints water
1 teaspoon sake (Japanese rice wine) or sherry (see Card No. 20)
1 teaspoon soy sauce; ¼ teaspoon monosodium glutamate
4 pieces yuzu or lemon peel

Prepare lobster and cut into 8 pieces. Soak mushrooms in warm water and when soft remove stalks. If fresh mushrooms are used, remove stalks and make a cut across each mushroom. Rub cucumber well with salt and cut into 8 ¼-inch slices. Remove the centre, and make a cut in one place in four of the slices. Slip each cut slice into one of the uncut slices, so that they will look like two rings linked together. Boil the water, add salt and the pieces of lobster and cook for 20 minutes. Remove lobster and sprinkle with sake. Strain the stock, and return 1¼ pints to the pan. Cook the cucumber for a few minutes in the remaining stock, remove and cook the mushrooms in the same stock. Put the lobster, cucumber and mushroom into a soup tureen. Add soy sauce, monosodium glutamate and salt to taste to the 1¼ pints stock in the pan. Bring to boiling point and pour into the tureen. Lastly add yuzu peel.

Oyster miso soup

Kaki no miso shiru

Preparation time	10 minutes
Cooking time	15 minutes
To serve	4

You will need

½ lb. oysters, weighed when removed from shells
5-inch piece of dashi kobu (if unavailable, add ½ teaspoon monosodium glutamate to water in which oysters are cooked)
½ lb. bean curd, cut in ¾-inch lengths
3½ tablespoons miso
4 asatsuki or chives, cut in ⅛-inch lengths

Wash oysters in salted water and drain. Put 1¼ pints water into a pan, add the washed dashi kobu if used. Heat to just below boiling point. Remove the dashi kobu. When water boils, add oysters, remove any scum and add bean curd. Bring to boiling point again. Mix the miso with a little of the hot liquid, then stir into the rest of the liquid. Bring to the boil, add asatsuki or chives and remove from the heat. Pour into bowls and serve hot.

Assorted raw fish
(Sashimi moriawase)

2

2 Assorted raw fish
Sashimi moriawase

Preparation time	40 minutes
Cooking time	0
To serve	4–6

You will need

½ cucumber
2 oz. daikon (Japanese radish)*
4 oz. tuna (optional)
1 squid (medium size)
½ sheet nori (dried seaweed)
3 chrysanthemum leaves
1 hard-boiled egg yolk
4 oz. sea bream
3–4 oz. smoked salmon in ⅛-inch slices**
5 lettuce leaves
4 fresh prawns
1 tablespoon wasabi, grated***
1 slice lemon
soy sauce

*Radishes, celery, cucumbers may be used instead.

**Smoked salmon is not a traditional Japanese food, but is used here because it tastes good. Salted salmon may also be used.

***Canned wasabi powder, mixed with the same quantity of water or horseradish may also be used.

Cut cucumber and daikon into thin strips. Soak separately in water for 20 minutes. Drain. Cut tuna, if obtainable, into ½-inch cubes and place on plate with daikon. Cut squid lengthwise at back and open. Remove legs and wash skin. Cut in half. Make cuts on the outside at ¼-inch intervals. Hold nori over heat for few minutes to crisp, and place on the side of the squid that is not cut. Roll from end like a Swiss roll. Cut into ¼-inch slices and place on plate. Cut the remaining half of the squid in thin strips. Arrange in a circle. Garnish with chrysanthemum leaves, placing egg yolk in centre. Clean and trim bream. Cut into ⅛-inch slices. Put on plate with cucumber. Put smoked salmon on plate with lettuce. Remove tails of prawns and reserve for garnish. Peel shell from remainder of prawns. Then remove veins. Cut into ¼-inch slices. Put into strainer, pour cold water over the prawns and drain. Serve with lettuce, garnished with the boiled tails. Grate wasabi or use wasabi powder and water or horseradish and put on lemon slice. Dip in soy sauce mixed with wasabi when eating.

Note Tuna fish is indispensable to Japanese cookery but when it is not available it could be omitted or replaced by mackerel marinaded in vinegar.

Grilled fish with miso
(Gyoden)

3

3 Grilled fish with miso
Gyoden

Preparation time	10 minutes
Cooking time	20 minutes
To serve	4

You will need

1 mackerel
4 tablespoons miso
2½ tablespoons sugar
2 tablespoons mirin (see Card No. 20)
½ cucumber
salt
1 tablespoon vinegar
4 radishes

Clean and trim mackerel and cut into about 8 slices. Mix the miso with 2 tablespoons water, add 2 tablespoons sugar and the mirin. Stir over gentle heat until it thickens to the original consistency of the miso.
Grill the mackerel for a few minutes, spread with the miso paste and finish cooking. Rub the cucumber with salt, and cut into 1½-inch pieces. Cut these in half lengthwise. Make cuts lengthwise at ⅓-inch intervals about 1¼ inches up each piece so that it will spread out like a fan.
Mix the vinegar with ½ tablespoon sugar and a pinch of salt and soak the pieces of cucumber in this for 1 minute. Cut the radishes into the shape of flowers and leave in cold water until they open out. Drain and sprinkle with salt. Arrange the mackerel and cucumber on a dish and garnish with the radishes.
Note The mackerel may be sautéed in a frying pan with a little salad oil.

Chicken on skewers
(Yakitori kushizashi)

4 Chicken on skewers
Yakitori kushizashi

Preparation time	30 minutes
Cooking time	30 minutes
To serve	4

You will need

4 chicken legs
6 tablespoons mirin (see Card No. 20)
6 tablespoons soy sauce
4 chicken livers
1 teaspoon ginger juice (powdered ginger may be used)
4 green peppers
3 tablespoons salad oil
salt
paprika
sansho powder or pepper

Wash and dry the chicken legs, cut into 1-inch pieces. Mix 4 tablespoons mirin with 4 tablespoons soy sauce and leave the pieces of chicken in this for 20 minutes. Drain and put on skewers. Reserve the sauce. Cut the livers in half, soak in water for 10 minutes, drain and wipe dry.
Mix 2 tablespoons mirin, 2 tablespoons soy sauce and the ginger juice and soak the livers in this for 20 minutes. Drain and put on skewers. Reserve the sauce. Cut the green peppers in four lengthwise, cut off the ends and remove the seeds. Sauté for a few minutes in the heated salad oil. Remove and sprinkle with salt and paprika. Put in the chicken, fry until brown, then cover and cook over low heat till tender. Remove from the pan. Sauté the chicken livers in the same way, adding a little extra oil if necessary.

Boiled chicken with dried mushrooms and bamboo shoots
(Tori no chikuzen-ni)

5 Boiled chicken with dried mushrooms and bamboo shoots
Tori no chikuzen-ni

Preparation time	30 minutes
Cooking time	40 minutes
To serve	4

You will need

8 oz. chicken meat
¼ lb. lotus root (if unavailable, use extra bamboo shoots)
5 oz. bamboo shoots, boiled
½ cake or ¼ lb. konnyaku (hydrosome rivieri) (optional)
¼ lb. carrots
salt
5 green beans
3 dried shiitake or 8 fresh mushrooms
6 tablespoons soy sauce
4 tablespoons sugar
3 tablespoons sake (Japanese rice wine) or sherry (see Card No. 20)

Cut chicken meat into ½-inch pieces. Peel lotus root and cut in quarters lengthwise, then cut into ½-inch slices. Soak in water for 10 minutes. Cut the bamboo shoots and konnyaku, if used about the same size as the lotus root. Boil the konnyaku and drain. Cut one piece of carrot about 1½ inches long and make into the shape of a flower. Cut the remainder into pieces the same size as the other vegetables and cook in boiling salted water. String the green beans, cut into 1½-inch pieces and cook in the water in which the carrots were cooked. Soften the shiitake in water, then cut into quarters. Heat 4 tablespoons soy sauce, 3 tablespoons sugar and 3 tablepoons sake in a pan. Put in the chicken and cook till tender. Remove the chicken and save the sauce. Heat 3 tablespoons oil in a pan, sauté the lotus roots for a few minutes, then add bamboo shoots, carrots, shiitake and konnyaku. Add the sauce left from the chicken and enough water to just cover the vegetables. Add remaining sugar and soy sauce. Cover, bring to boiling point, then reduce the heat and cook until the sauce has reduced by about ⅓. Add the chicken and continue to cook until the sauce has evaporated. Turn the chicken frequently during this process. Arrange the chicken on a serving dish, garnish with the carrots, green beans and the carrot 'flower'.

Bean curd and cabbage rolls
(Tofu iri kyabetsumaki)

6 Bean curd and cabbage rolls
Tofu iri kyabetsumaki

Preparation time	10 minutes
Cooking time	30 minutes
To serve	4

You will need

8 cabbage leaves
salt
8 × 10 inch strips kampyo (dried gourd strip) or 8 cocktail sticks
10 oz. bean curd
4 tablespoons negi or leek, finely sliced
¼ lb. minced beef
2½ tablespoons sugar
5 tablespoons soy sauce
1 egg
1 pint chicken stock
1 tablespoon cornflour
thinly sliced rind of ½ lemon

Remove leaves from cabbage one by one without tearing them. Cook in boiling salted water till tender. Drain and remove stump. Soak kampyo in water until it softens. Drain bean curd. Put negi or leek into a pan with the meat, add ½ tablespoon sugar and 1 tablespoon soy sauce and cook over low heat. When cool, add bean curd and lightly beaten egg and mix well.
Divide into 8 portions and roll in cabbage leaves. Secure with strips of kampyo or cocktail sticks. Arrange the rolls in a pan, pour over the stock and add remaining sugar and soy sauce. Bring to boiling point, then reduce heat and simmer for 30 minutes. Add cornflour mixed smoothly with 2 tablespoons water and cook till the sauce thickens.
Arrange the rolls on a serving dish, pour the sauce over and garnish with the lemon peel.

7 Mackerel soup
Sembajiru

Preparation time	1 hour
Cooking time	30 minutes
To serve	4

You will need

½ lb. mackerel fillets
salt
2 oz. daikon (Japanese radish) or radishes
5 inches dashi kobu (kelp)
1½ pints water
2 tablespoons sake (Japanese rice wine)
¼ teaspoon monosodium glutamate
1 teaspoon vinegar
1 tablespoon asatsuki, finely chopped or spring onion

Cut mackerel fillets in 4. Sprinkle with 2 tablespoons salt and stand for 1–2 hours. Cut daikon into slices ¼-inch wide and 2-inches long. Wash mackerel, pour over boiling water, then wash again with cold water. Place mackerel in a pan with daikon, dashi kobu, water and sake. Bring to boiling point, then remove dashi kobu. Reduce heat and simmer for 20 minutes, removing any scum as it rises. Add monosodium glutamate, vinegar and salt to taste. Pour into a tureen and sprinkle with finely chopped asatsuki or spring onion.

Note This is a soup made with daikon and salted mackerel. It got its name 'semba jiru' because it was first made in a port area of Osaka called 'Semba'.

Steamed egg custard with vegetables (Chawan-mushi)

8 Steamed egg custard with vegetables
Chawan-mushi

Preparation time	20 minutes
Cooking time	30 minutes
To serve	4

You will need

4 eggs
1⅛ pints stock
salt
2 teaspoons mirin (see Card No. 20)
1½ teaspoons soy sauce
¼ teaspoon monosodium glutamate
3 oz. very thinly sliced chicken
4 dried shiitake (dried Japanese mushroom) or canned mushrooms
4 prawns
4 oz. white fish
½ teaspoon sake (Japanese rice wine) (see Card No. 20)
4 green beans

Beat the eggs well, add stock, 1 teaspoon salt, 1 teaspoon mirin, ½ teaspoon soy sauce and ¼ teaspoon monosodium glutamate. Strain into a basin. Put chicken on to a plate, add 1 teaspoon mirin and 1 teaspoon soy sauce and leave for 5 minutes. Soak shiitake in water till soft, then drain, if mushrooms are used, slice thinly. Peel and devein the prawns and cut in half. Shred the fish and sprinkle with the sake and a little salt. Slice the green beans thinly in a slanting direction. Cook in boiling salted water and drain. Divide the chicken, shiitake, prawns, fish and green beans equally between 4 fireproof dishes. Pour the egg mixture over, cover with greased paper and steam until the custard has set (about 20 minutes).

Note This is a hot dish in which chicken, shiitake, green beans, fish, prawns, etc. are steamed together in an egg mixture. It can be made from canned crab meat only with the egg mixture. Also, instead of steaming each serving separately, it can all be put in a casserole together and baked in the oven as a baked custard.

Scallops and cucumber salad
(Kai to kyuri no sunomono)

Lobster salad with egg dressing (Ise-ebi kimizu kake)
Steamed aubergines with sesame seeds (Nasu goma-ae)

9 Lobster salad with egg dressing

Ise-ebi kimizu kake

Preparation time	30 minutes
Cooking time	30 minutes
To serve	4

You will need

2 cooked lobsters
salt
vinegar
2 sticks celery
2 egg yolks
¼ teaspoon monosodium glutamate
½ teaspoon sugar
1 teaspoon katakuri or cornflour

Separate the body from the head of the lobster. Cut the under shell with scissors and remove the lobster meat without breaking the shell. Slice the meat into pieces about ⅛-inch thick, sprinkle with a little salt and vinegar, then replace in the shells. Put the heads back into position. Cut the celery in 1½-inch lengths, then slice lengthwise very thinly. Put into cold water for a little while to crisp, then drain, place on serving dish and put lobsters on top. Put the egg yolks into a double pan with the monosodium glutamate, sugar, ¼ teaspoon salt, 2 tablespoons vinegar and the katakuri or cornflour mixed smoothly with ¼ pint water. Stir constantly until the sauce thickens. Check seasoning and pour over lobster.

Scallops and cucumber salad

Kai to kyuri no sunomono

Remove the hard white part of ½ lb. scallops. Peel off the thin skin. Wash with salted water. Cut across into 4 slices. Sprinkle with a little vinegar. Rub cucumber with salt and wash in cold water. Cut into 1½-inch lengths. Then cut in half lengthwise. Make thin cuts into the cucumber from the outside without cutting through. Sprinkle with salt. Squeeze lightly and wash with water. Squeeze again. Sprinkle with 1 teaspoon vinegar and press again to remove as much moisture as possible. Arrange on a dish with the scallops. Sprinkle the scallops with grated wasabi and garnish with watercress. Mix 2 tablespoons vinegar and 1 tablespoon water with ½ teaspoon soy sauce, 1 tablespoon sugar and ¼ teaspoon monosodium glutamate. Mix well and pour over the scallops and cucumber.

Steamed aubergines with sesame seeds

Nasu goma-ae

Slice 1 aubergine (about ¼ lb.) thinly into pieces about 2 inches long and ¼ inch wide. Leave in cold water for 10 minutes, then cook till tender in boiling salted water. Drain and press lightly to squeeze out the water. Put 5 tablespoons sesame seeds into a thick hot pan and stir till they swell and begin to snap, then grind with a pestle and mortar. Do not roast them too much. Add 3 tablespoons soy sauce, 2 tablespoons sugar and ¼ teaspoon monosodium glutamate, pound together. Add to the aubergine and mix well.

10 Vegetable tempura and recipe for tempura batter

Preparation time 20 minutes
Cooking time 20 minutes
To serve 4

You will need

½ lb. sweet potatoes; 1 small carrot; 12 green beans
2 green peppers; 4 chrysanthemum leaves
oil for frying; 6 oz. flour; 1 egg
¼ pint dashi or ¼ pint water with ½ teaspoon monosodium glutamate
4 tablespoons soy sauce
4 tablespoons mirin or sherry
4 tablespoons grated daikon or horseradish

Peel the sweet potatoes, cut into ½-inch thick slices and leave in water for 10 minutes, then drain well. Peel the carrot, cut in half, then in ¼-inch slices lengthwise. Make cuts at ¼-inch intervals leaving ½-inch uncut at the bottom. String the beans and cut in half. Cut peppers in half lengthwise, remove stem and seeds. Wash and dry chrysanthemum leaves. For the batter: Mix the flour with the beaten egg and 6 tablespoons water. Add a little more water if the batter is too thick. Coat the back of the chrysanthemum leaves with the batter and deep fry for a few minutes in hot oil. Drain and fry all the vegetables in the same way. Put the dashi into a pan with the soy sauce and mirin and bring to the boil. If sherry is used add a little sugar. Serve tempura with grated daikon and sauce in which vegetables are dipped.

Variation: Kushi-age

Preparation time 40 minutes
To serve 4

You will need

8 button onions; salt
8 large canned mushrooms
16 shrimps; ¼ lb. chicken meat
½ teaspoon ginger juice or ground ginger
2 teaspoons sake
2 green peppers; ¼ lb. white fish
6 oz. flour; 1 egg
¼ pint dashi or ¼ pint water with ½ teaspoon monosodium glutamate
4 tablespoons soy sauce; 4 tablespoons mirin or sherry
4 tablespoons grated daikon or horseradish
oil for frying

Cut both ends from onions and parboil in boiling salted water. Drain mushrooms well. Shell and devein shrimps. Cut chicken into 1-inch squares about ⅓ inch thick. Sprinkle with ginger juice and sake. Cut green peppers lengthwise. Remove stem and seeds and cut in pieces about same size as the chicken. Cut fish about the same size and sprinkle with ginger juice. Arrange all on skewers. Make the batter with the flour, beaten egg and water and the sauce as for vegetable tempura. Have the oil heated on the table. Dip the skewers in the batter and then fry as for fondue. Dip in grated daikon and the dipping sauce before eating.

Rice with beef and eggs
(Itoko-domburi)

11 Rice with beef and eggs
Itoko-domburi

Preparation time 5 minutes
Cooking time 10 minutes
To serve 4

You will need

3/8 pint stock
4 tablespoons sake (Japanese rice wine) (see Card No. 20)
4 tablespoons soy sauce
2 tablespoons sugar
I small onion, sliced thinly
1/2 lb. thinly sliced beef
4 eggs
8 oz. rice, cooked
4 asatsuki or spring onions
1 sheet nori (dried seaweed, optional)

Put the stock, sake, soy sauce, sugar and onion into a frying pan and bring slowly to boiling point. Put in the meat and cook until the meat changes colour and is tender. Add the beaten eggs and tilt the pan so that the whole surface is covered with the egg. Cover and cook for 2-3 minutes until the eggs are just set.

Place the rice in 4 serving bowls and put 1/4 of the egg and meat mixture in each. Sprinkle with asatsuki. If nori is used, hold it over heat for a few minutes to crisp, put in a cloth and rub so that it crumbles and then sprinkle over the beef and egg mixture.

Note Chicken and eggs on rice is called Oyako-domburi (parent and child bowl) and beef and eggs on rice is called Itoko-domburi (cousin bowl). When pork is used it is called Tanin-domburi (stranger bowl). Thinly sliced boiled bamboo shoot can also be used. Each serving may be made separately in a frying pan or the 4 servings may be cooked together and then divided.

12 Fish rice

Taimeshi

Preparation time	10 minutes
Cooking time	40 minutes
To serve	4

You will need

1 lb. rice
1½ pints water
4 tablespoons sake (Japanese rice wine) (see Card No. 20)
½ teaspoon salt
3½ teaspoons soy sauce
½ lb. sea bream or turbot
3 tablespoons sugar
1 sheet nori (dried seaweed)

Prepare the rice 1 hour before cooking. Wash and put into a thick pan with the water, 2 tablespoons sake, ¼ teaspoon salt and 1½ teaspoons soy sauce. When ready to cook, bring to boiling point; reduce the heat, cover and cook for 10–12 minutes. Turn off heat and leave to stand for 15 minutes, then put into a bowl. While rice is cooking, cook the bream in boiling salted water. Drain, remove skin and bones, wrap in a cloth and rub lightly until the fish flakes. Put the fish into a pan with the sugar, 2 tablespoons sake, 2 teaspoons soy sauce and pinch of salt. Cook, stirring briskly to prevent the fish sticking, until it becomes dry. Put the fish over the rice. Hold the nori over the heat for a few minutes to crisp, then cut in thin strips and sprinkle over the fish.

Variation

Chrysanthemum rice balls

Kikka nigiri

Preparation time	10 minutes
Cooking time	45 minutes
To serve	4

You will need

1 lb. rice; ½ lb. sea bream or turbot
3½ tablespoons sugar
2 tablespoons sake (Japanese rice wine); salt
red food colouring (cochineal); 1 egg
¼ teaspoon salad oil; chrysanthemum leaves

Cook rice as in fish rice. Cook bream in boiling salted water. Remove skin and bone, wrap in a cloth and rub lightly until the fish flakes. Put 3 tablespoons sugar, 2 tablespoons sake and pinch of salt into a pan. Add a few drops of cochineal and the fish and cook, stirring briskly to prevent sticking until the fish is dry. Beat the egg, add pinch of salt, ½ tablespoon sugar and salad oil. Put into a pan and scramble. Divide the rice into 12 portions and roll into balls. Wring a cloth tightly out of cold water. Divide the fish into 12 portions. Put one portion on the cloth and one ball of rice on top. Gather up the ends of the cloth and squeeze tightly. Make an indentation in the centre of the ball with the finger, then remove the cloth. Fill the hole with scrambled egg, press together. Make other balls in the same way. Arrange on a plate, garnish with chrysanthemum leaves.

13 Tricolour rice
Miiro domburi

Preparation time	10 minutes
Cooking time	40 minutes
To serve	4

You will need

1 lb. rice
1 pint water
3½ tablespoons soy sauce
salt
3 tablespoons sake (Japanese rice wine) (see Card No. 20)
1 teaspoon chopped fresh ginger (optional) or 1 teaspoon chopped spring onion
4½ tablespoons sugar
1 tablespoon mirin
7 oz. minced chicken
2 eggs
¼ teaspoon monosodium glutamate
6 oz. peas
little pink ginger (optional)
4 sprigs watercress

Wash and drain the rice. Put into a pan with the water, 1½ tablespoons soy sauce, ¼ teaspoon salt and 3 tablespoons sake and leave for 1 hour. Then bring to boiling point, reduce the heat, cover and cook for 10 minutes. Turn off heat and leave for 15 minutes without removing the lid. Put into a bowl.

While rice is cooking, put chopped ginger or spring onion into a pan with 1½ tablespoons sugar, mirin, 2 tablespoons soy sauce and chicken. Stir constantly with a fork till chicken is cooked and liquid absorbed. Beat the eggs, add pinch of salt, 1 tablespoon sugar and monosodium glutamate. Put into a pan and scramble. Cook the peas in ⅓ pint boiling water to which ½ teaspoon salt and 2 tablespoons sugar have been added. Leave until cool, then drain. To serve arrange chicken, eggs and peas on the rice. Put watercress and pink ginger round the edge.

Note This is a beautiful and colourful rice dish, using minced chicken meat, scrambled eggs, green peas. It is ideal to serve for lunch.

14 Tokyo sushi rice

Nigirizushi

Preparation time	1 hour
Cooking time	40 minutes
To serve	4

You will need

1 lb. rice; 1½ pints water
salt; 4 tablespoons vinegar
2 teaspoons sugar; monosodium glutamate
4 prawns; or 8 shrimps
2 large scallops
Japanese omelette (see Card No. 15)
4 thin slices sea bream or halibut
4 thin slices tuna (see Note of Card No. 2)
4 thin slices smoked salmon
¼ cucumber
2 sheets nori (dried seaweed)
1 tablespoon grated wasabi or horseradish
1 slice lemon; watercress

Wash rice 1 hour before cooking and drain. Cook in boiling salted water for 10 minutes. Raise heat for 1 second, then remove from heat and leave for 12 minutes. Put into a large wooden or ordinary bowl, and sprinkle with the vinegar mixed with 1 teaspoon salt, 2 teaspoons sugar and ¼ teaspoon monosodium glutamate. Remove heads from prawns, shell, leaving tail part and devein. Sliver inner side with knife and open. Sprinkle with salt. Stick a cocktail stick in the inner side of shrimps so they will not curl. Remove hard white part of scallops, skin and wash in salt water. Cut each into 4 slices. Cut Japanese omelette in ½-inch slices. Cut bream and smoked salmon into 1 – 2-inch slices. Rub cucumber with salt, cut into 4 pieces lengthwise, sprinkle with salt. Hold nori over heat for a few minutes to crisp, cut each sheet in half. Put one piece of nori on a dry cloth and spread with rice about ¼-inch thick leaving a ½-inch edge. Put a pinch of wasabi on top, then roll over, as if bending it in half. Put a second piece of nori on the cloth, spread with rice as before, place cucumber in the centre, sprinkle with wasabi and roll over. Cut the rolls into 4 – 6 pieces using a knife dipped in vinegar. Sprinkle 2 slices of scallop with wasabi and place a ball of rice on top, and press with the fingers. Put on to a damp cloth and press into shape. Cut strips from the remaining nori and wrap round this sushi (sandwich). Repeat this process with the prawns, slice of omelette and fish. Garnish smoked salmon ones with lemon, and omelette ones with watercress. Arrange on a dish and serve with sweet vinegared ginger if available.

Omelette roll
(Dashimaki tamago) **15**

15 Omelette roll
Dashimaki tamago

Preparation time	5 minutes
Cooking time	10 minutes
To serve	4

You will need

½ cucumber
salt
6 eggs
3 tablespoons sugar
1 tablespoon mirin (see Card No. 20)
6 tablespoons dashi or water to which ¼ teaspoon monosodium glutamate has been added
salad oil
lettuce

Rub the cucumber with salt. Pour on boiling water, then rinse with cold water. Drain, and cut into three pieces. Cut each lengthwise into 4 and sprinkle with salt. Beat 3 eggs lightly, add half the sugar, half the mirin and 3 tablespoons dashi. Heat some oil in a frying pan, pour in ⅓ of the egg mixture, and as soon as it begins to set, roll up away from yourself towards the edge of the pan. In the space liberated, fry the second ⅓ of the egg mixture, rolling it round the first pancake. Brush the pan with a little more oil, fry the rest of the mixture, rolling the pancake round the first two. Remove from the pan and wrap in a cloth. Repeat the process with the other 3 eggs. When cold, cut each roll in 4 and arrange on a bed of lettuce. Garnish with the cucumber.
Note This is a Japanese omelette.

16 Sukiyaki

Preparation time	15 minutes
Cooking time	0
To serve	4

You will need

½ lb. shirataki or fine vermicelli
1 stick celery
6 oz. bamboo shoots
2 leeks
8 spring onions
1 small can mushrooms
1–1½ lb. very thin slices raw tender beef
little beef fat
Warishita:
½ pint dashi or water with ½ teaspoon monosodium glutamate
7 tablespoons soy sauce
7 tablespoons mirin or sherry
2–3 tablespoons sugar
(if sherry is used, add a little extra sugar)
4 eggs, optional

Cook shirataki or vermicelli in boiling salted water, drain and cool. Cut celery, bamboo shoots, leeks, onions and mushrooms into short lengths, slantwise. Put on a large plate with the beef. Put all the ingredients for the warishita together in a pan. Bring to boiling point and pour into a gravy boat. Heat a heavy pan and rub the bottom with a little beef fat. Cook enough beef for the first serving, add a little of the Warishita and vegetables. Each portion should be eaten as it is cooked and can be dipped in the beaten egg if liked. The Sukiyaki is generally cooked at the table by each guest like a fondue.

Full moon udon (Tsukimi-udon)
Udon with duck (Kamonamban)

17 Full moon udon

Tsukimi-udon

Preparation time	5 minutes
Cooking time	30 minutes
To serve	4

You will need

10 oz. dried udon or noodles; 2 negi or leeks
6 tablespoons soy sauce; 2 tablespoons mirin (see Card 20)
½ tablespoon sugar; salt
1¾ pints chicken stock; 4 eggs
shichimi togarashi (pepper powder mixture) or pepper

Put the noodles into a pan with plenty of boiling salted water. Stir, and when water boils again, add ¼ pint cold water. Bring again to boiling point and add another ¼ pint cold water. Remove a piece of the udon and break it. If it is chalk white inside, it is cooked. Remove from the pan, rinse with warm water and drain. Cut enough of the green part of the negi into thin slices to give about 2 tablespoons. Cut the white part into thin slices slantwise. Put the chicken stock into a pan, add soy sauce, mirin, sugar and salt to taste. Bring to boiling point. Put the udon into 4 individual marmites or fireproof dishes. Put the white 1 part of the negi on top. Pour the hot soup over. Break an egg into the centre of each and put into a moderate oven (350° F, or Gas Mark 4) for a few minutes to set the egg. Sprinkle with the green part of the negi and a little shichimi togarashi or pepper.

Udon with duck

Kamonamban

Preparation time	5 minutes
Cooking time	30 minutes
To serve	4

You will need

10 oz. dried udon or noodles; 2 negi or leeks
6-inch piece of dashi kobu; 1½ pints water with ½ teaspoon monosodium glutamate
5 tablespoons soy sauce; 2 tablespoons mirin
½ tablespoon sugar; salt
½ lb. thinly sliced raw duck meat

Cook udon as described in recipe for full moon udon. Wash and drain. Cut the green part of the negi into thin slices, and the white part into thin slanting pieces. Put the dashi kobu into a pan with the 1½ pints water. Heat and remove the dashi kobu just before the water boils. Remove any scum from the stock and measure out ½ pint. Put this into a pan with soy sauce, mirin, sugar and salt to taste. Bring to boil, add slices of duck and cook till tender. Remove and keep hot. Add the remaining stock to the liquid left in the pan and bring to boiling point. Add the white part of negi and re-boil. Put the udon or noodles into a strainer and pour over boiling water to heat them, then drain and put into a bowl. Put the duck on top. Pour the soup over and sprinkle with green negi.

Fluffy snow kanten
(Awayuki-kan)

18 Fluffy snow kanten

Awayuki-kan

Preparation time	30 minutes
Cooking time	20 minutes
To serve	4

You will need

1 kanten (agar)
12 oz. sugar
1 egg white
½ teaspoon grated lemon rind
1 tablespoon lemon juice
4 strawberries (optional)

Wash the kanten and squeeze out the water. Add ¾ pint water and leave for 30 minutes. Cook over low heat until all the kanten has melted, then strain through muslin. Put this liquid into a pan with the sugar and cook over medium heat until the quantity is reduced by half. Remove any scum as it rises. Beat the egg white stiffly, add lemon rind and juice and beat gradually into the cooked kanten adding a little at a time. Mix well and leave until it begins to thicken, then pour into a wetted or lightly oiled 6-inch square mould or tin and leave to set. Turn out and cut into 8 pieces. Place half a strawberry on each piece.

19 Potato and chestnut buns

Kurikanoko

Preparation time	30 minutes
Cooking time	30 minutes
To serve	4

You will need

½ lb. sweet potatoes
3 oz. sugar
pinch salt
10 cooked fresh chestnuts or canned whole chestnuts

Peel sweet potatoes thickly. Cut into ¼-inch slices and soak in water for 30 minutes. Put in saucepan and add water to cover. Boil until the potato becomes soft. Drain. While still hot add 1 oz. sugar and mash. Rub through a sieve then add remaining sugar and salt. Stir with wooden spatula or spoon over heat until the mixture becomes firm. Cool and then make into 4 balls. Cut chestnuts in half from top to bottom. Press 5 halves into each potato ball.

Dashi and wakame seaweed soup 20

20 Dashi

Soup stock

Japanese people use dashi for stock. It is made with bonito and dashi kobu (kelp). The bonito is grated to very fine flakes. As this is unavailable in Western countries, chicken stock, fish stock or monosodium glutamate were substituted here. When stock is made in Western countries, different kinds of seasonings are used, but in Japanese cooking, the only seasoning used is negi and sometimes ginger. This kind of simple stock suits the Japanese palate.

Sake:

Japanese rice wine is used here, but sherry is similar in taste and can be used instead.

Mirin:

This is sweet wine. 1 teaspoon sugar added to 1 tablespoon sherry makes it taste like mirin.

Amount of seasonings:

The amounts given here suits the Japanese palate. If desired, the amount of sugar, soy sauce, salt may be adjusted to your own taste.

Ingredients:

Ingredients peculiar to Japan have been substituted by canned foods or ingredients available in other countries.

Wakame seaweed soup

Preparation time	10 minutes
Cooking time	20 minutes
To serve	4

You will need

¼ oz. dried wakame (edible seaweed)
½ lb. white fish
salt
1 teaspoon sake (Japanese rice wine)
1 tablespoon cornflour
½ pint boiling water
1¼ pints fish stock*
1 teaspoon soy sauce
yuzu peel (or lemon peel)

Soften wakame in water. Cut off the hard part in centre. Cut remaining wakame to 2-inch pieces. Cut fish into pieces about ¼ inch thick. Sprinkle with a little salt and sake, and stand for 10 minutes. Coat with cornflour. Put into boiling water piece by piece and boil. Heat fish stock. Add salt to taste and wakame. When soup boils, add 1 teaspoon soy sauce. Monosodium glutamate will improve the taste. Place fish and wakame in soup bowls. Pour hot soup on top. Put a small piece of yuzu peel in for fragrance.

* Soup stock taken from dashi kobu (kelp) and dried bonito flakes is better, but when making stock with fish, only use onion for seasoning.